PEAK DISTRICT HIGH LEVEL ROUTE

BY

JOHN N. MERRILL

Maps and Photographs by John N. Merrill

A J.N.M. PUBLICATION

1987

a J.N.M. PUBLICATION

JNM PUBLICATIONS,
WINSTER,
MATLOCK,
DERBYSHIRE.
DE4 2DQ

Conceived, edited, typeset, designed, marketed and distributed by John N. Merrill.

© Text and route—John N. Merrill 1983 and 1987

© Maps and photographs—John N. Merrill 1987

First Published—September 1983
Reprinted June 1984
This revised and enlarged edition—June 1987

ISBN 0 907496 55 5

(ISBN 0 907496 10 5 Ist Edition)

Meticulous research has been undertaken to ensure that this publication is highly accurate at the time of going to press. The publishers, however, cannot be held responsible for alterations, errors or omissions, but they would welcome notification of such for future editions.

Printed by: Richard Bates Limited, Southmoor Road, Wythenshawe, Manchester M23 9NR

ABOUT JOHN N. MERRILL

John combines the characteristics and strength of a mountain climber with the stamina and athletic capabilities of a marathon runner. In this respect he is unique and has to his credit a whole string of remarkable long walks. He is without question the world's leading marathon walker.

Over the last ten years he has walked more than 60,000 miles and successfully completed ten walks of at least 1,000 miles or more.

His six major walks in Great Britain are:
Hebridean Journey .... 1,003 miles
Northern Isles Journey .... 913 miles
Irish Island Journey .... 1,578 miles
Parkland Journey .... 2,043 miles
Lands End to John o'Groats .... 1,608 miles
and in 1978 he became the first person (permanent Guinness Book of Records entry) to walk the entire coastline of Britain—6,824 miles in ten months.

In Europe he has walked across Austria—712 miles, hiked the Tour of Mont Blanc, completed High Level Routes in the Dolomites, and the GR20 route across Corsica in training! In 1982 he walked across Europe—2,806 miles in 107 days—crossing seven countries, the Swiss and French Alps and the complete Pyrennean chain—the hardest and longest mountain walk in Europe with more than 600,000 feet of ascent!

In America he used the the world's longest footpath—The Appalachian Trail -2,200 miles—as a training walk. He has walked from Mexico to Canada via the Pacific Crest Trail in record time—118 days for 2,700 miles.

During the summer of 1984, John set off from Virginia Beach on the Atlantic coast, and walked 4,226 miles without a rest day, across the width of America to Santa Cruz and San Francisco on the Pacific Ocean. This walk is unquestionably his greatest achievement, being, in modern history, the longest, hardest crossing of the USA in the shortest time—under six months (178 days). The direct distance is 2,800 miles.

Between major walks John is out training in his own area — the Peak District National Park. As well as walking in other parts of Britain and Europe he has been trekking in the Himalayas five times. He has created more than ten challenge walks which have been used to raise more than £250,000 for charity. From his own walks he raised over £80,000. He is author of more than seventy books, many of which he publishes himself. His next major walk—2.400 miles—is down the length of New Zealand.

CONTENTS

INTRODUCTION

With my major walks in different parts of the world into high and rugged places, it seemed logical to create something along these lines on my door step. The more I looked at the Peak District, the more it became obvious how apt a high level route would be because of its terrain. The area geologically is known as the Derbyshire Dome, with gritstone covering the limestone rock. Millions of years ago a huge upheaval pushed the rock upwards demolishing the gritstone and exposing the limestone. It is for this reason that we have the gritstone outcrops (edges) on the eastern and western fringe of the area. In the middle are the limestone dales.

With this in mind I began looking at the area closely with the aim: "to encircle the Peak District via its highest and rugged places." I later added "my favourite places." Fot the better part of a year I kept making forays into the high places using new footpaths to me. By August 1983 I had walked all the route in segments and had selected the paths to use. My aim here was to use as many paths as possible that were little used.

In late August I set off to walk the route in its entirety over four days. The weather was kind - just bright sky, warm sun and no rain. Here in one fell swoop I walked across and over many of my favourite places and kept high all the time, with extensive views. As I neared Matlock I felt a deep sadness that the walk was about to end. Now at last I have a remote but hard walk on my doorstep!

The route is a challenging one but I hope you follow my footsteps and enjoy one of the perfect walking areas of England.

Happy walking,

John N. Merrill.

JOHN N. MERRILL.

1

HOW TO DO IT

MAPS:— O.S. Tourist Map - Peak District - covers whole route

The following cover the route in great detail -
O.S. 1:25,000 Outdoor Leisure Map - The White Peak
O.S. 1:25,000 Outdoor Leisure Map - The Dark Peak

The Hathersage area is only covered by -
O.S. 1:50,000 Sheet No. 110 - Sheffield and Huddersfield

O.S. 1:25,000 Sheet No. SK 28/38 will cover the Hathersage area in great detail.

The route is circular and both ends and starts from Matlock, because of its good communications network. However, there is no criterion for starting it there and you can join the route anywhere.

On my final full circuit I did the walk comfortably in four days from Matlock, stopping at Butterton, Taxal and Ladybower. There is no need to do it in that kind of time scale and the route is laid out into six stages. You can even take longer if you wish! There are ample places to stay, camp or hostel on the the route and plenty of places for a backup party to meet you. You could for instance use Bakewell as a base and be ferried out each day to the continuation point.

You will need to carry a couple of days food for there are several long high level traverses where shops or inns are non existent. But this is one of the joys of the route; you are high and away from everything.

A master record of "high level" walkers is kept by me. Badges and signed certificates are available from J.N.M.Publications to all who complete the walk.

By the end of 1986 several hundred people have completed the walk either in one expedition or over several weekends. The universal response has been—"super walk"; "I must say how much I have enjoyed it"; and "very good with very good views". I couldn't agree more!

ABOUT THE WALK

I decided the walk should start from Matlock; not just because I have a flat there but because it has good communications - train, bus and close to the M1 motorway. Matlock is also just outside the National Park and has numerous hotels and a Youth Hostel.

The route is almost in a circle and is walked clockwise - to do it anticlockwise is the Devil's way! From Matlock you ascend straight away and begin a traverse of the limestone country via a whole string of attractive villages. In fact the first twenty miles are the most populated with numerous inns and shops - later there will be nothing for miles. From Matlock you cross to Bonsall and Brassington before gaining the dolomitic limestone of Harborough Rocks. More limestone is crossed to the outstanding village of Tissington and to reach Ilam you skirt Dovedale.

From Ilam, the end of the first stage, you begin heading northwards into remote and higher country of Grindon and Butterton. You are also entering the gritstone country. The Hill, the finest all round vantage point on the route, is the start of a magnificent high walk via the Mermaid Inn to the spectacular Roaches. After crossing these you descend to the river Dane which you follow towards its source and Three Shires Heads. Here the three counties you walk in meet - Cheshire, Staffordshire and Derbyshire. Leaving the river just to the north of here you ascend onto the spine of the hills and ridge walk to the Cat & Fiddle Inn, Shining Tor, Cats Tor and to Windgather Rocks.

From the rocks you begin swinging east to Taxal, Buxworth Canal Basin and over Chinley Churn to Hayfield. Here begins a hard but short traverse of the southern perimeter of the Kinder Plateau before descending to Hagg Farm. To reach the next main high traverse line - the gritstone edges - you first cross beneath Crook Hill before gaining Moscar and the start of Stanage Edge. Here you begin my favourite traverse to Longshaw, Froggatt, Curbar, Baslow and Birchens Edge.

The final section still keeps to high ground as you pass Chatsworth Edge, Dobb Edge, to the Hunting Tower above Chatsworth, and past Swiss Lake to Beeley Hill Top. The end is not far as you still hug the valley sides of the Derwent to Fallange and Northwood. Here you leave the heights and descend to the valley floor and for the final four miles into Matlock you walk close to the Derwent via Darley Bridge and Oaker.

3

MATLOCK TO BRASSINGTON — 7 Miles

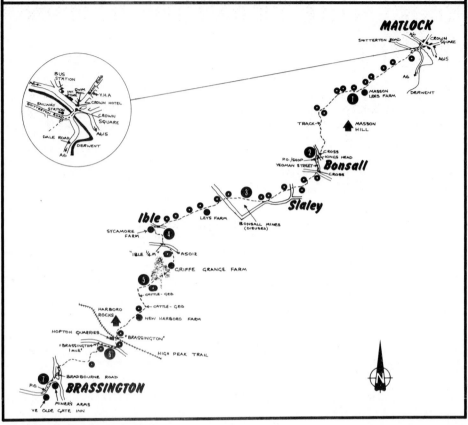

HARBOROUGH ROCKS

MATLOCK TO BRASSINGTON — 7 Miles

ABOUT THE SECTION —

Hilly route across the limestone fringe of the National Park, passing several villages and an outcrop of dolomitic limestone rock.

MAP: O.S. 1:25,000 Outdoor Leisure Map - The White Peak.
— East Sheet.

WALKING INSTRUCTIONS —

From Crown Square, in Matlock, follow the A6 road over the river Derwent. Just after the bridge bear right up Snitterton Road, passing Royal Bank of Scotland on your right and a flower shop on your left. Just beyond at the entrance to Bridge Farm turn left onto the signposted footpath - Bonsall. After a few yards you reach an open field, which you ascend directly on a well defined path. At the end cross a lane passing a footpath sign - Bonsall via Masson Hill 1½ miles. Continue on the defined path keeping the field boundary on your left. Pass through several stiles before approaching Masson Lees Farm, ½ mile away. Pass it on the right and at the top of the field is a stile and track beyond. Turn right and after 20 yards bear left, gently ascending around the fringe of a quarry to a stile and another shortly afterwards before a track. Turn right down the track for 20 yards to a stile on your left. Cross the field to a gap before walking between two widely spaced walls for two fields. Pass through two stiles before bearing right to a track. Turn left along this. At first it is simply a grassed track. Later it becomes walled and as you near Bonsall it is a concrete walkway. After ¼ mile bear left on the track and follow it all the way to Bonsall, entering the village beside the cross and King's Head Inn.

Descend through Bonsall along Yoeman's Street. After ¼ mile at the next cross, turn right then left onto the stiled and stepped path. Ascend the steps and follow the path as it bears right then left to a stile on your right. Two more stiles later, bear right across to another stile and follow the stiled path across the fields above Slaley. Just over ¼ mile later you reach a minor road. Turn right and leave the road 5 yards later to reach another stile. The path is faint but all the fields have good stiles that act as guidelines as you weave your way past the remains of leadmine shafts. After ½ mile you reach the same minor road again. Again cross over and keep the wall on your immediate left as you cross the fields to the northern side of Leys Farm. Cross more fields; all well stiled, to Ible village ½ mile away. Turn right along the minor road into the village, passing the Methodist Chapel and watertroughs on your right. On your left is Sycamore Farm. Turn left, and although not obvious as a right of way, descend the drive and keep left of the houses.

After 100 yards turn sharp left and cross the field to a stile under a bush. Turn right and descend into woodland. 100 yards later you reach the A5012 road and path sign - Ible ¼ mile. This particular right of way is little used but you should have no trouble finding your way.

THE START: CROWN SQUARE, MATLOCK

MATLOCK

Cross the road and ascend the farm drive to Grange Farm. Pass through the farmyard and bear left along the track into woodland. In the wood bottom bear right along the track which gently ascends to a gate at the wood's eastern perimeter. Continue on the track for another 100 yards to another gate and track. Turn left along this and after the second cattle-grid, turn right and keep the wall on your right as you ascend to New Harboro Farm. Just before the farm buildings ascend the ladder stile on your right and walk past the farm on your left to a stile. Ascend more steeply now to a stile and cross the summit of Harbour Rocks — dolomitic limestone. Descend to the High Peak Trail, which you cross, and walk down the lefthand side of Hopton Quarries. At the road turn right and walk past the factory buildings and ¼ mile later on your left is the stile and path sign — Brassington 1 mile. Keep the wall on your left as you walk around the field before descending to a stile at the end of a lane. Turn right and walk along the lane for almost ½ mile. Turn left onto the minor road and after the village hall right onto the Bradbourne Road and into central Brassington.

BONSALL CROSS

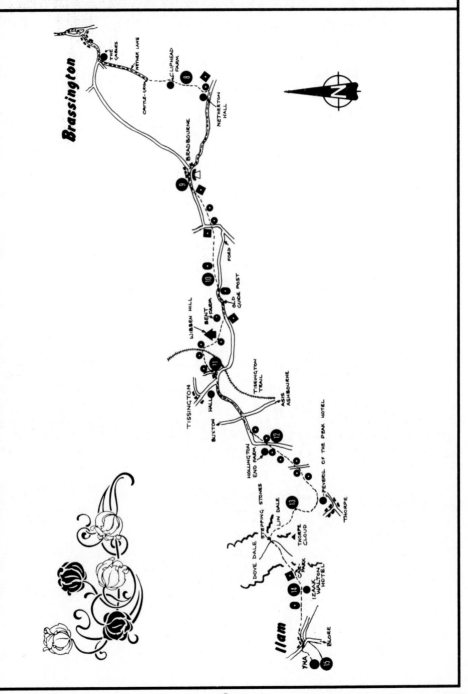

BRASSINGTON TO ILAM — 8 Miles

ABOUT THE SECTION —

You continue your traverse of the limestone plateau via Bradbourne to the attractive village of Tissington. Two miles later you skirt the village of Thorpe and descend Lin Dale to the entrance of Dove Dale. You can make a slight detour here and ascend Thorpe Cloud. The final mile is across the fields to Ilam and into Staffordshire.

MAPS: O.S. 1:25,000 Outdoor Leisure Map - The White Peak.
East sheet up to Dove Dale. West sheet beyond.

WALKING INSTRUCTIONS —

From Brassington follow the Bradbourne road, past Ye Olde Gate Inn and Post Office on your right. About 100 yards later at the Gables on your left, turn left along the No Through Road — Nether Lane. For the next ½ mile you keep on this hedged lane. Immediately after the second cattle-grid leave the track and begin crossing the fields to the lefthand side of Clipshead Farm. Just beyond the farm you bear left and cross three fields to a stile, footpath sign — Brassington — and the minor road close to Netherton Hall. Turn right and follow the road for just over ½ mile to Bradbourne village. Turn left at the road junction just past the Post Office. Past the telephone kiosk on your left and at the end of the houses, on your left is the footpath sign and stile. Descend the stiled fields, keeping near the road to the B5056 road. Cross over, as footpath signed, and begin heading for Tissington village. First cross the stream via the bridge on your left before heading up the field to a fence — no stile here. Bear right up the next field to a gate and shortly afterwards reach the Tissington road. Walk along this for ¼ mile passing the small plantation on your right known as Bent Dumble. On your left is an old mile post. Just past the entrance to Bent Farm, turn right, as footpath signed, and cross the field to a gate on the left of Wibbin Hill. At a stile beyond bear right to another stile and the Tissington Trail. Cross this and ascend the steps and follow the stiled path into Tissington. Turn left and just after the telephone kiosk right along the path by the houses to central Tissington and village pond.

Keep to the road to your left as it curves out of the village, along a tree lined avenue to Tissington Gates and the A515 road. Cross the road and walk along the minor road towards Thorpe. After ¼ mile turn left and cross a foot-bridge then stile and cross the field to the road again, opposite the entrance to Hollinton End Farm. Opposite is the stile and path sign - Thorpe ¾ mile. The path is defined and well stiled as you cross four fields to a minor road. Turn left then right onto another footpath signed path. Again well stiled as you walk beneath Hamston Hill and past Peveril of the Peak Hotel on your left. Just beyond the hotel you turn right past a small quarry on your right and begin descending Lin Dale to the river Dove and stepping stones. Above rises Thorpe Cloud and a slight detour takes you to its summit and magnificent view. Cross the stepping stones and bear left along the road to the car park, ¼ mile away. Here as footpath signposted, turn right and begin crossing

HARBOROUGH ROCKS

YE OLDE GATE INN, BRASSINGTON

the fields to Ilam; first skirting past the Izaak Walton Hotel. The path is well used and well stiled. Beyond the hotel is a kissing gate before gradually descending to the road and gate on the edge of Ilam. Bear right and at the cross right. At the entrance to Ilam Hall turn left onto the path to the church then Hall.

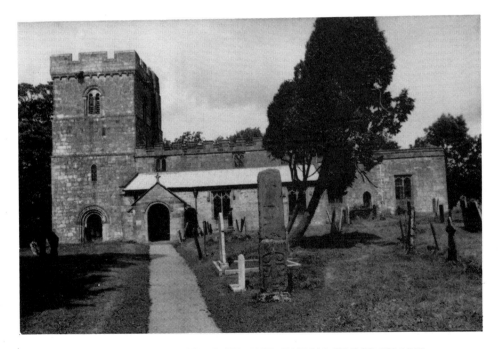

BRADBOURNE CHURCH AND SAXON CROSS SHAFT

LONDON MILE POST, NR. TISSINGTON

TISSINGTON — VILLAGE POND

DOVEDALE STEPPING STONES

ILAM CHURCH

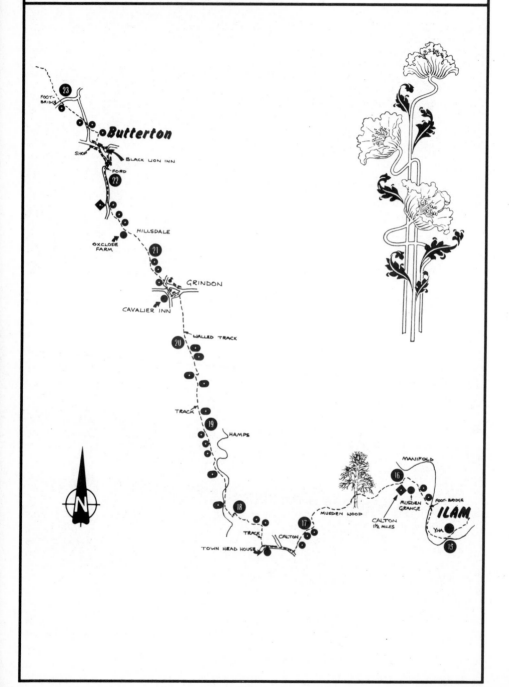

ILAM TO THE HILL — 8 Miles

ABOUT THE SECTION —
Leaving the southern edge of the walk and limestone country, you cross the Hamps valley to gain high country around Grindon and Butterton. The view from The Hill is one of the finest on the whole walk.

MAP: O.S. 1:25,000 Outdoor Leisure Map - The White Peak - West Sheet.

WALKING INSTRUCTIONS —

From Ilam walk past the Hall and Youth Hostel and down to the Minfold river. Turn right and walk along "Paradise Walk". Approximately ½ mile from the hall you reach the footbridge over the river. Turn right over this and follow the path across the field to a stile. After this turn right and follow the ascending path to the right of Musden Grange before descending to a stile and minor road. Turn left and walk along the road. Where it turns left for Musden Grange, turn right onto the track and path through Musden Wood. The path sign states - Calton 1½ miles. For the next mile walk through woodland on a defined path. Leave the western edge of the wood via a stile and continue ahead on the path with the field wall on your left. It is well stiled and just over ¼ mile you reach the road on the outskirts of Calton. Turn right along it, keeping straight ahead at the road junction 100 yards later. 130 yards later the road turns sharp left at Town Head House. Here turn right onto a walled track. Follow this for ¼ mile - it is a bit overgrown in places - to a stile on your left. Descend the hillside via the stiles and walk along a walled track for 100 yards before descending the three fields to the tarmaced path beside the river Hamps; reached by a gate.

Turn right and walk along the valley floor for just over ¼ mile until opposite Lee House. On your left is a wooden kissing gate. Pass through this and bear right and ascend a track in woodland to a gate. Continue on out of the trees and pass a barn on your right before ascending the field to a stile on your left. Further stiles lead you past another barn before gaining a track. Bear right along this to a farm ½ mile away. Walk past the farm and descend the track as it zig-zags down into a small dale. Ascend out of it and keep the wall on your left to a gate and then another before gaining a walled track. Follow this into Grindon ½ mile away. Just before entering the village at the junction of tracks turn left to the Cavalier Inn.

Walk past the inn and a few yards later turn right for Grindon church. Bear left as you near it along the tarmaced road and almost opposite it is the stile - set back from the road. Ascend this and keep the field boundary on your left to reach another two stiles. After the last stile you begin descending to Oxclose Farm. Walk round the righthand side of the buildings to the road. Cross it to the stile and again keep the field boundary on your left as you cross the fields to the stiles. At the end of the fifth field you reach the minor road from Butterton. Turn right and descend this first to a ford then into Butterton and Black Lion Inn.

Just past the inn turn left beside the church, walk along the village road towards the local shop. Just before it turn right at Croft Head Farm and ascend past the house to the field; at the top of which is the stile. Turn left and ascend the stile and cross two further stiled fields to the minor road. Turn right and one field later on your

GRINDON CHURCH

BLACK LION INN — BUTTERTON

left is a wooden stile. Ascend this and cross two fields before keeping the field wall on your left to the minor road from Warslow. Ahead can be seen the trig point on The Hill. Cross the road to a stile and keep the field wall on your right and descend to a footbridge. Keep to the lefthand side of Hill Farm before bearing left after a water trough to a stile then a marshy area before the farm track close to Hole. Turn left along the track and right down beside Hole on a track. Follow it as it curves left to a gate. Keep the field boundary on your right as you descend close to pine trees down to a footbridge before Ryecroft. Walk through the farm and bear left beside a fence to another footbridge. Keep the fence on your right as you walk around the field perimeter. At the wall bear left and ascend to the right of the farm - Under the Hill. Ascend the stile and cross the farm track to another stile. You now ascend in earnest up The Hill; first to a wooden stile and then to the summit and its unsurpassed view.

MERMAID INN

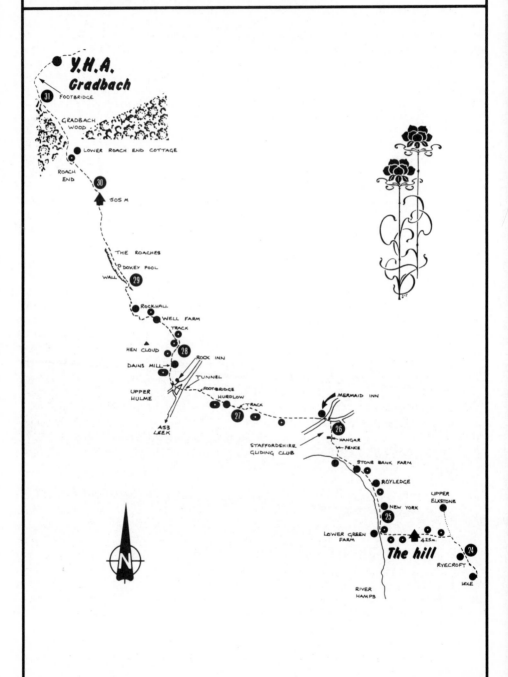

Y.H.A.
Gradbach

31 FOOTBRIDGE

GRADBACH WOOD

LOWER ROACH END COTTAGE

ROACH END

30

505 M

THE ROACHES

DOXEY POOL

WALL

29

ROCKHALL

WELL FARM

TRACK

HEN CLOUD

28

ROCK INN

DAINS MILL

TUNNEL

FOOT-BRIDGE

UPPER HULME

HURDLOW

27 TRACK

A53 LEEK

MERMAID INN

26

HANGAR

STAFFORDSHIRE GLIDING CLUB

FENCE

STONE BANK FARM

ROYLEDGE

UPPER ELKSTONE

NEW YORK

25

LOWER GREEN FARM

425 m.

The hill

24

RYECROFT

HOLE

RIVER HAMPS

N

THE HILL TO GRADBACH — 8 Miles

ABOUT THE SECTION —

You walk up to the source of the river Hamps and to the Mermaid Inn. The view from here is extensive and ahead can be seen your route to Upper Hulme and over The Roaches. Once over these you descend to the river Dane and Gradbach.

MAP: O.S. 1:25,000 Outdoor Leisure Map - The White Peak - West sheet.

WALKING INSTRUCTIONS —

Descend due west from the Hill to a stile. Cross the minor road to another stile and descend close to a track on your right, for two fields to the river Hamps. Turn right past the ford at Lower Green Farm and head northwards across the fields. The path line is faint but the stiles are all there. First you pass near the farm called New York on your right. Two fields later pass Royledge side of Stone Bank Farm. Just beyond you reach the now infant river Hamps. Here turn right, keeping the fence on your right as you curve round to your left to a gate. Here you head due north past a hangar on your left as you cross the Staffordshire Gliding Club field. At the road turn left to the minor road and the Mermaid Inn.

Turn left and at the gate on your right just past the inn's car park, turn right through the gate and angle left as you descend across a large field, keeping just above a ravine. Just beyond is the stile. Continue descending to a gate close to a small wood on your left. Turn left and gain the track which takes you through Hurdlow farm. 100 yards later leave the track and bear right to the prominent foot-bridge. Over this ascend to your right then left and walk through a tunnel beneath the A53 road. Ascend the field beyond and descend a stone stile well to the right of a farm on your left. In front of you is the Rock Inn. Turn left down the road, then right into the bottom of Upper Hulme. Cross the stream and turn right up the concrete drive heading for Dains Mill. 75 yards later after a gate bear left down the track to the ruined mill. Walk round the lefthand side of it and follow the stiled path close to the stream. After two stiles and just before a solitary barn, turn left to a stile. Ascend this and reach the track. Turn left then right and walk along the track to Well Farm.

Walk through the farm to a stile and cross the field to The Roaches Estate. Turn left at the track and right soon afterwards past Rockhall and ascend to the rocks. Turn left along the path beneath them and 300 yards later ascend onto the summit and turn left. For the next 1½ miles you walk along the crest of The Roaches, past Doxey Pool and trig point 505 metres. Descend to the road at Roach End. Go through the stile at the start of the track to Lower Roach End Cottage, and turn right keeping the wall on your right. You gradually descend for ¼ mile on a good path to the start of Gradbach Wood. Pass through the beech trees and descend on a distinct path through the pine trees. At the first path junction keep right and at the next left. All the time the Black Brook is below you on your right. After ½ mile through the wood you reach a foot-bridge on your right. Cross this and follow the stiled path with the river Dane on your left. ¼ mile later you reach Gradbach Mill which is now a Youth Hostel.

THE ROCK INN — UPPER HULME

THE ROACHES AND MAIN OVERHANG

GRADBACH YOUTH HOSTEL

WINDGATHER ROCKS

GRADBACH TO WINDGATHER — 9 Miles

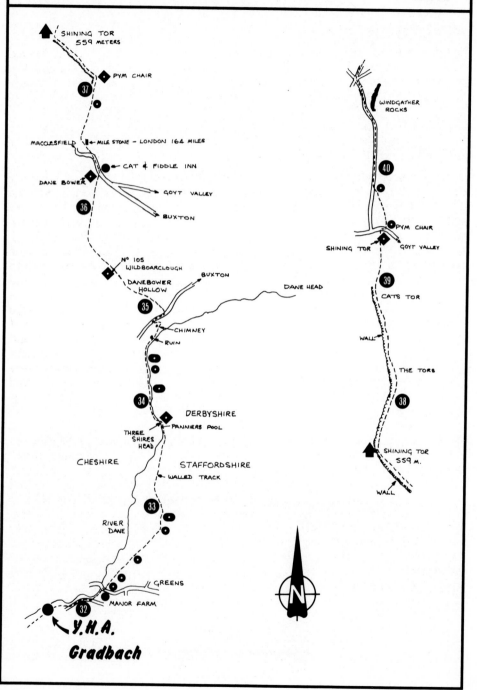

SHINING TOR
559 METERS

PYM CHAIR

37

MACCLESFIELD — MILE STONE - LONDON 164 MILES

CAT & FIDDLE INN

DANE BOWER

GOYT VALLEY

36

BUXTON

No 105
WILDBOARCLOUGH

DANEBOWER
HOLLOW

BUXTON

DANE HEAD

35

CHIMNEY

RUIN

34

DERBYSHIRE

PANNIERS POOL

THREE
SHIRES
HEAD

CHESHIRE

STAFFORDSHIRE

WALLED TRACK

33

RIVER
DANE

GREENS

32

MANOR FARM

Y.H.A.
Gradbach

WINDGATHER
ROCKS

40

PYM CHAIR

SHINING TOR

GOYT VALLEY

39

CATS TOR

WALL

THE TORS

38

SHINING TOR
559 M.

WALL

N

GRADBACH TO WINDGATHER — 9 Miles

ABOUT THE SECTION —

First you cross the fields near the river Dane to reach Three Shire Heads. Beyond you ascend Danebower Hollow and cross the moorland to the Cat & Fiddle Inn. From here you commence a high level traverse over Shining Tor with views of the Cheshire Plain and Jodrell Bank, to Windgather Rocks.

MAPS: O.S. 1:25,000 Outdoor Leisure Map - The White Peak - West sheet.

WALKING INSTRUCTIONS —

From the hostel walk up the drive to the road and turn left. There is a path on your left that avoids this bit of road walking. After 200 yards turn left over the footbridge and cross the field to the road on the left of Manor Farm. Turn right and left almost immediately over the stile. Just beyond on your right is another stile and footpath sign. Continue ahead keeping the wall on your left as you gently ascend five fields. In the fifth field the wall ends but keep straight ahead to a stile. Ahead can be seen a ladder stile and once over this bear left to a gate and wall which curves round to your left to a stile. Just after this gain the walled track and turn left along it and follow it for the next ½ mile to the packhorse bridges over the river Dane. Cross the second bridge to the lefthand side of the river and turn right, following a public bridleway. Basically you keep the river on your right for the next ¾ mile to a ruined building on your left. Here you leave the now infant river and ascend to the righthand side of a chimney. Turn left through the gate and reach the A54 road. Turn right and 50 yards later left onto the wide path up Danebower Hollow; keeping the fence on your right. Little over ½ mile later pass footpath sign No. 105 - Wildboarclough - on your left. Just over ½ mile later you reach the A537 road opposite the Cat & Fiddle Inn.

Turn left along the road for 100 yards before keeping straight ahead on the Emerald Farm Road. A short distance along this track on your right is an old mile stone - London 164 miles. Shortly afterwards keep right as you maintain height. ½ mile later ascend a ladder stile before turning left on the footpath - Pym Chair. Keep the wall on your left as you ascend to the summit of Shining Tor. The actual trig point is on private property but access to it is via a stile. You now head almost due north along the spine of the hill with the wall on your left. For the next couple of miles you follow this high route past The Tors and onto Cats Tor before reaching the road at Pym Chair. Turn right then left over two ladder stiles and continue northwards over the moorland. ¼ mile later reach the road via a stile. Turn right and walk along it for the next mile to Windgather Cottage, with Windgather Rocks on your right.

THREE SHIRES HEADS AND PACKHORSE BRIDGES

CAT & FIDDLE INN

MILESTONE — NEAR CAT & FIDDLE INN

THE CHIMES OF TAXAL

WINDGATHER TO HAYFIELD — 7 Miles

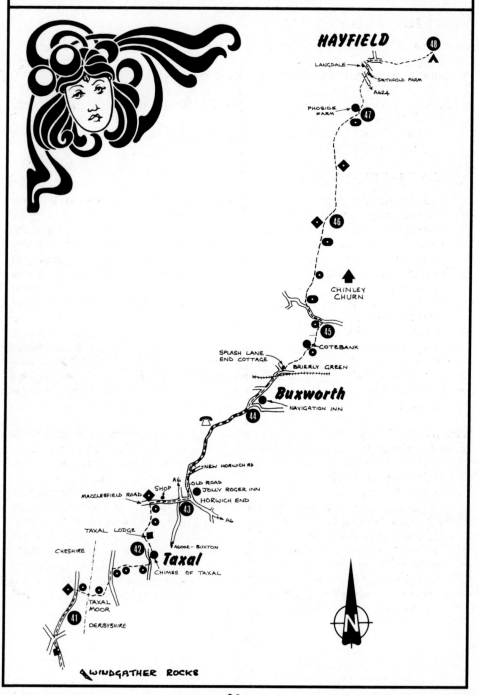

HAYFIELD

48

LANGDALE

SMITHFOLD FARM

A624

PHOSIDE
FARM

47

46

CHINLEY
CHURN

45

COTEBANK

SPLASH LANE
END COTTAGE

BRIERLY GREEN

Buxworth

44

NAVIGATION INN

NEW HORWICH RD

A6

SHOP

OLD ROAD

JOLLY ROGER INN

MACCLESFIELD ROAD

HORWICH END

43

A6

TAXAL LODGE

A6002 - BUXTON

CHESHIRE

42

Taxal

CHIMES OF TAXAL

TAXAL
MOOR

41

DERBYSHIRE

N

WINDGATHER ROCKS

WINDGATHER TO HAYFIELD — 7 Miles

ABOUT THE SECTION —

After crossing Taxal Moor you descend to Taxal and Whaley Bridge. A short road walk brings you to the impressive Buxworth canal basin before the ascent and traverse of Chinley Churn. A short descent from here brings you to Hayfield.

MAP: O.S. 1:25,000 Outdoor Leisure Map - The White Peak - West sheet - details the route to Taxal.
O.S. 1:25,000 Outdoor Leisure Map - The Dark Peak - details the route from Taxal to Hayfield.

WALKING INSTRUCTIONS —

From Windgather Cottage continue along the road to the five-ways junction. Turn right but not sharp right onto the signposted path. Follow the road for just over ¼ mile to the stile and path just beyond the third building on your right. Ascend the path to a stile and footpath sign and cross Taxal Moor to a ladder stile. Shortly afterwards bear left on the descending path to the minor road. Turn left along this beside the pine trees to a ladder stile on your right. Ascend this and descend the well stiled path to Taxal, little over ¼ mile away. At the village road turn left, passing the church on your right. Leave the road and walk in front of the Chimes of Taxal on a footpath. This path leads past Taxal Lodge and across the fields to the A5002 Macclesfield Road. You reach the road opposite Reddis Road. Turn right and descend to the cross roads and A5002 Buxton road. Cross over and walk up Chapel Road. 75 yards later turn left past the Jolly Roger Inn, along Old Road. Less than ¼ mile later turn right up New Horwich Road and after 30 yards left down a walled path emerging onto a road in front of the church. Turn right and follow this road for the next ¾ mile to Buxworth and its Canal Basin.

Walk past the Navigation Inn on your right and past a school on your right. Walk under the railway line and past Dolly Lane on your left. Just after the shop on your left, turn left and walk past Splash Lane End Cottage and ascend the stiled path to Cotebank. Keep to the right of the buildings and pass through the stiles and after ¼ mile reach the minor road. Turn left along this for 120 yards. Just past the entrance to Throstle Bank bear right onto the walled track to a gate. Follow this walled track across the moorland on the west side of Chinley Churn. It is well stiled and gated. After ½ mile pass a bridlepath sign on your left. ¼ mile later you come to a triple bridlepath sign. Keep straight ahead with the wall on your left and still on a track. After another ¼ mile turn right and descend to Phoside Farm on a stiled path. At the farm descend the farm track to the A624 road. Cross over and walk past Smithfold Farm. At the road beyond turn left and opposite Langdale House right down a walled path. At the road turn right and ½ mile later is the campsite.

BUXWORTH CANAL BASIN

FOOTPATH SIGN No. 3 NEAR TUNSTEAD HOUSE

EDALE CROSS

LADYBOWER INN SIGN

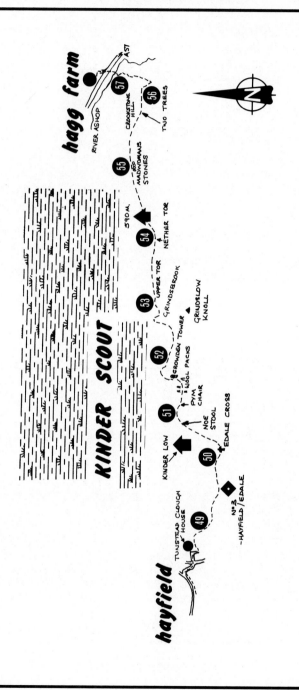

HAYFIELD TO HAGG FARM — 10 Miles

ABOUT THE SECTION —

After a gradual ascent from Hayfield to Edale Cross you traverse the southern edge of Kinder Scout to Crookstone Hill - all a magnificent high level route. A short descent across the river Ashop brings you to Hagg Farm.

MAP: O.S. 1:25,000 Outdoor Leisure Map - The Dark Peak.

WALKING INSRUCTIONS —

From the entrance to the campsite in Hayfield, keep to the righthand side of the Kinder river, following the public bridleway to Edale Cross. At first it is a tarmaced road which swings to your right before the entrance to Tunstead Clough Farm. As footpath signed ascend the track to the farm, bearing right around it before ascending due east up the stiled path. At the fourth stile turn right as footpath signed - Edale Cross - to a kissing gate. The path is well used as you cross another field to another kissing gate. After this you bear left to a ladder stile and Open Country. Bear right and soon join another path coming in from your left as you gradually ascend towards the cross. Close to Stony Ford you pass footpath sign No. 3 - Hayfield to Edale. Continue on to the cross where you turn left and ascend to the wall. Here turn right and walk beneath Swine's Back to join a wide path, which is your companion for the next few miles.

You now begin your high level traverse of Kinder as you contour round the plateau's edge, first to the prominent Noe Stool and onto Pym Chair and the Wool Packs. Next you come close to Crowden Tower before crossing the Pennine Way and Grindsbrook. Bear right here and keep to the perimeter edge as you walk above Grindsbrook to Nether Tor. Just after these rocks you leave the edge and head for the prominent trig point - 1,937 ft. There is a path to this and on to your next object - Madwoman's Stones. Just after these bear right (do not head for the summit of Crookstone Knoll) and follow the path to a wall and the perimeter again. Shortly afterwards you turn right and descend past a small quarry on your left as you follow a well defined track over the slopes of Crookstone Hill to a gate. Beyond at two trees, bear left, as footpath signposted to a stile and boundary of Open Country. Turn right along the track with the wall on your left. At the footpath cross-roads, turn left - signposted Haggside 1 mile. The track leads down first beside the forest on your right to a gate and into the trees. After the first righthand bend in the track you cross a small stream. Here turn left and descend the path between the widely spaced trees to Haggwater Bridge. Cross the bridge and ascend to the A57 road. Cross this and ascend the track for Hagg Farm, signposted - Derwent Dale 1½ miles, After 75 yards, turn left to the hostel and campsite.

HAGG FARM TO SURPRISE VIEW
12 Miles

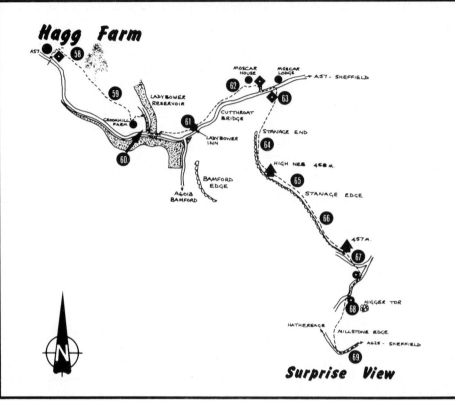

Hagg Farm

MOSCAR HOUSE
MOSCAR LODGE
A57 - SHEFFIELD

LADYBOWER RESERVOIR

CUTTHROAT BRIDGE

CROOKHILL FARM

LADYBOWER INN

STANAGE END

HIGH NEB 458 M.

STANAGE EDGE

BAMFORD EDGE

A6013 BAMFORD

457 M.

HIGGER TOR

HATHERSAGE
MILLSTONE EDGE

A625 - SHEFFIELD

N

Surprise View

LADYBOWER RESERVOIR

32

HAGG FARM TO SURPRISE VIEW
12 Miles

ABOUT THE SECTION —

After a short crossing of Crook Hill you descend to Ladybower reservoir. Here you begin the ascent onto Stanage Edge; the start of the gritstone edges. You traverse the whole of Stanage before walking close to Millstone Edge, to Surprise View - a magnificent view up the Hope Valley to Mam Tor.

MAP: 1:50,000 Sheet No. 110 - Sheffield and Huddersfield - covers whole route.
O.S. 1:25,000 Outdoor Leisure Map - The Dark Peak - covers Hagg Farm to Ladybower Reservoir.
O.S. 1:25,000 Sheet No. SK 28/38 - covers whole section.

WALKING INSTRUCTIONS —

Walk down the drive of Hagg Farm and turn left to the gate and ascend the track which zig-zags its way up to a cross-roads of paths. Turn right onto the public bridleway and walk along a track with the pine plantation on your left. After ½ mile you gain a gate and another public bridleway sign. Continue ahead to a ladder stile, leaving the woodland behind as you cross the pastures in front of Crook Hill. Ascend another ladder stile and begin following a grass track beneath the hill to Crookhill Farm. Here turn left and descend the farm road to the minor road above Ladybower Reservoir. Turn right and left onto the A57 road and cross Ashopton Viaduct. At the other end turn left onto the Water Board road, bearing right past the houses to a gate. Keep on the track and follow it to your right as it becomes a very pleasant grass track as it winds its way past the Ladybower Inn on your right after ½ mile - there is a path down to it! Continue on the track as it ascends across heather moorland, first to near Cutthroat Bridge and then onto Moscar House. Before the house you reach path sign No. 75 - Derwent Edge to Derwent. Here you turn right to cross the field to the track just before Moscar Lodge and another path sign No. 88. Turn right and at the A57 road left. 100 yards later, turn right at the footpath sign and ascend onto Stanage Edge.

For the next four miles you walk along the summit of Stanage Edge to High Neb and the trig point 457m near Cowper Stone. Just before the pillar you leave the edge and follow the defined path to the road. Cross this to a stile and cross the field to another stile and road beneath Higger Tor. Turn right and ascend the second stile on your left. This takes you first to a clump of trees and then across to Millstone Edge. Gain a track here and walk along this to the A625 road. Turn left to Surprise View.

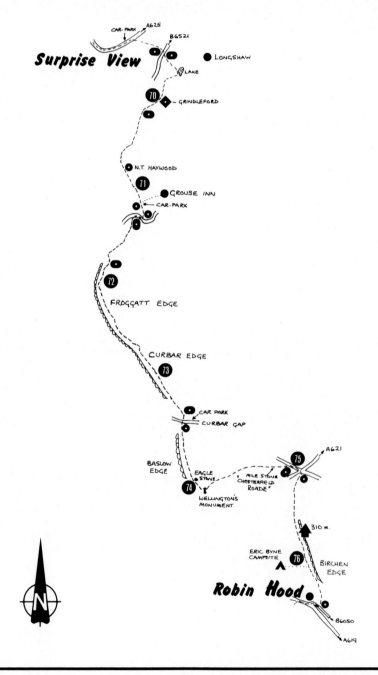

SURPRISE VIEW TO ROBIN HOOD
8 Miles

ABOUT THE SECTION —
Basically maintaining your height you hug the lip of the Derwent valley and walk through pleasant woodland through Longshaw to Froggatt Edge. For the next five miles gritstone edges are your companion as you walk onto Curbar, Baslow and above Gardom's Edge to Birchen's, Robin Hood Inn and Eric Byne Campsite.

MAP: O.S. 1:25,000 Outdoor Leisure Map - The White Peak - East Sheet.

WALKING INSTRUCTIONS —

Continue around the road from Surprise View (A625) towards Sheffield. Just past Surprise View car park on your left, leave the road via the stile on your right and walk down the sunken path to the footbridge over the Burbage Brook and ascend to the gate and road - B6521. Cross over to the stile and walk into Longshaw on the well defined path to the lake. At the southern end of the lake, where the track turns sharp left into the rhododendrons, turn right and walk on a faint path through the pine trees. After about 150 yards you reach a distinct track; turn left along this. About 150 yards later bear right - as footpath signposted - Grindleford. This high level path weaves its way along the valley side with views down onto Padley and railway line. After ½ mile the path turns sharp right and descends; don't descend here but keep straight ahead and descend to a small brook. Cross this and ascend the faint path beyond through the trees to a wide track. Bear right along this to Tedgeness Road and path sign - Froggatt Edge Road. Turn left and left again on the signposted path - Froggatt Edge. After a stile you enter Haywood National Trust property. Continue ascending gently through the trees and pass the car park on your left after ½ mile. Descend to a stream, cross it and ascend to the road - B6054.

Cross the road to the kissing gate and track leading onto the top of Froggatt Edge. For the next two miles you follow this well defined path along Froggatt Edge and later Curbar Edge. Descend to a kissing gate then the minor road at Curbar Gap. Cross the road and ascend to the ladder stile. Again you have a well defined track to follow across the moorland above Baslow Edge. After ½ mile reach the Eagle Stone, where you turn left to Wellington's Monument. Turn left at the monument and follow the track for the next mile to a minor road, reached by a gate. Turn right and cross the A621 road to the ladder stile. Ascend this into Open Country, once more, and follow the path to Birchen Edge ½ mile away. Walk past the rocks and descend to the road and Robin Hood Inn. At the rocks on your right is the ladder stile and path to the Eric Byne campsite.

OLD MILLSTONES — STANAGE EDGE

EAGLE STONE

ROBIN HOOD INN SIGN

HUNTING TOWER — CHATSWORTH

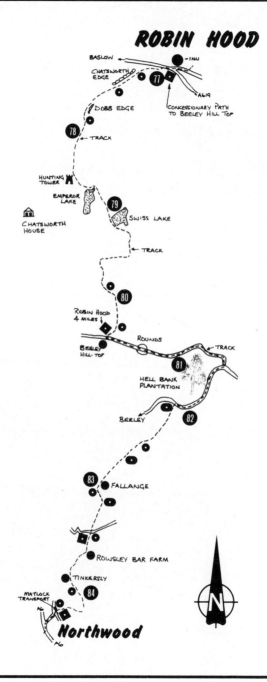

ROBIN HOOD TO MATLOCK — 13 Miles

ABOUT THE SECTION —

The final lap! First you follow a high level concessionary path above Chatsworth House before descending to Beeley Hill Top. A short ascent returns to high ground as you traverse round to Fallange and Rowsley Bar. From here rather than get enmeshed in the sprawl of villages close to Matlock you descend to the valley floor and river Derwent. The final four miles follow its course back to central Matlock.

MAP: O.S. 1:25,000 Ourdoor Leisure Map - The White Peak - East Sheet.

WALKING INSTRUCTIONS —

Descend to the main road - A619 - from the Robin Hood Inn. Turn right and 20 yards later cross over to your left to the footpath sign - Concessionary Path - Robin Hood to Beeley Hill Top. Descend the steps and cross the stream via the log footbridge and ascend to the track. Cross this to the solitary stone footbridge and follow the path beside the pine trees to the ladder stile. The path is well defined for the next ½ mile as you walk above Chatsworth Edge and cross the fields to Dobb Edge. Just beyond you ascend a stile and turn sharp left to a track. Turn right along this and after 100 yards you pass a footpath sign on your left - Concessionary path to Beeley. Just over ¼ mile later turn left on the track and left again, passing the Hunting Tower in the trees on your right. You are now following the yellow arrowed route to Beeley. Keep on the track as you skirt the northern end of Emperor Lake and walk through Stand Wood to Swiss Lake. Keep on the track past this before following the track as it bears right and right again ¼ mile later. After another ¼ mile the track swings left and after a cross roads of tracks you bear left into beech trees and a stile. Ascend this and follow the track beyond for 100 yards before turning right and descending the well defined path to Beeley Hilltop.

At the walled track close to the farm, turn left and ascend this for a mile, passing through the circle of trees known as - Rounds. The track curves round the perimeter of Hell Bank Plantation. Upon reaching the minor road turn right and descend it for ½ mile to the footpath sign on your left. Leave the road here and pass through two gates before following the gated path, keeping the wall on your left for four fields. In the fifth field bear right to the righthand side of a barn. Again keep the wall on your left for two more fields before going through a gate and keeping the wall on your right. Walk past a ruined farm on your right before reaching Fallange. Pass through two gates before heading for the stone stile in the corner. Ascend this to another stile infront of a large farm building. Bear right past the building onto the farm road. Turn left and walk up the farm road to a gate. Continue on the track as it turns right. Where it turns sharp left a few yards later, keep straight ahead, with the wall on your right to a gate. In the corner of the next field is a crude stile before a minor road.

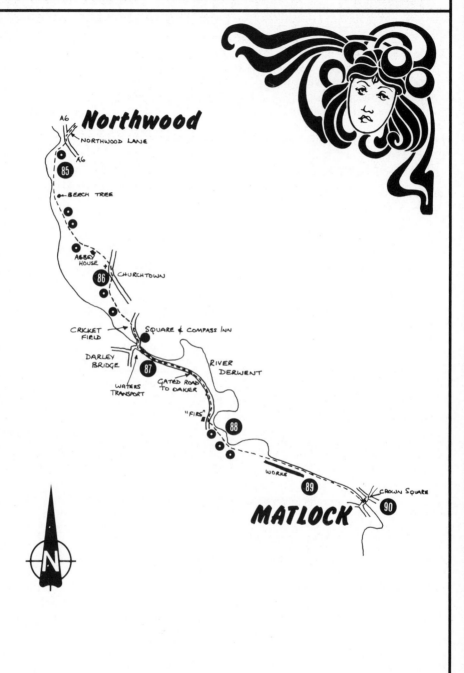

A6

Northwood

NORTHWOOD LANE

A6

85

BEECH TREE

ABBEY HOUSE

86

CHURCHTOWN

CRICKET FIELD

SQUARE & COMPASS INN

DARLEY BRIDGE

87

RIVER DERWENT

WATERS TRANSPORT

GATED ROAD TO DAKER

"FIRS"

88

WORKS

89

CROWN SQUARE

90

MATLOCK

N

Cross the road and follow the public bridleway along the track to Rowsley Bar Farm. Here you turn right and begin the descent from the heights. Keep the wall on your right as you gain a tarmaced lane. Continue ahead towards Tinkersley passing a footpath sign - Rowsley Bar. Just beyond the lane turns right. Keep straight ahead to a stile and cross the subsequent field to another stile on the edge of woodland. Walk into the wood and after 100 yards turn right and descend the path which soon reaches a brook and swings round to your right to a stile. Don't cross the footbridge on your left but continue ahead to a wooden stile and enter the yard of the Matlock Transport Company. Descend to the road and footpath sign. Turn left then right and descend Northwood Lane to the A6 road. On your right is Orchard Cafe.

Turn left and right almost immediately to the banks of the river Derwent. Turn left and follow the path beside the river. After 100 yards you ascend a stile and leave the riverside and begin crossing the fields on a track. In the fourth field you approach the river again before passing a solitary beech tree on your left before reaching the stone stile 120 yards away. Cross the next field to a stile on the right of a barn. Keep the wall on your left to another stile, then track past Abbey House and into Churchtown. On reaching the road just before the church, bear right past St. Helens church. At the end of the graveyard on your right is the gate and footpath for Darley Bridge. Cross the first field passing close to a private house on your left before reaching the stile. Bear left around the next field to another stile and track. On your right is the cricket field.

Upon reaching the B5057 road, turn right along it to the bridge over the Derwent, passing your last inn on the route - The Square and Compass on your left. On the other side of the bridge and in front of Waters Transport yard, turn left along the gated road to Oaker. For the next mile you walk along this to the fringe of Oaker. Follow the road round above the river Derwent to the start of the houses. Opposite the "Firs", turn left on to the footpath down to the river. Follow this stiled path beside the river for three fields before walking beside a fence and past an industrial complex on your right. You are now into your final mile of the walk! After ¼ mile you leave the factory behind and keep to the riverside on a tarmaced path that leads eventually into a car park just before the A6 bridge over the Derwent in central Matlock. Turn left over the bridge and 30 yards later is Crown Square where the walk began.

Congratulations on completing the high level walk!

JOHN N. MERRILL.

ST. HELEN'S CHURCH, CHURCHTOWN, DARLEY DALE

LAST INN! — SQUARE & COMPASS — DARLEY BRIDGE

42

AMENITIES GUIDE

Village Town	B & B	YHA	Camp-site	Inn	Restau-rant	Shop	P.O.
MATLOCK	★	★	★	★	★	★	★
BONSALL	★			★		★	★
BRASSINGTON	★			★		★	★
TISSINGTON	★						
THORPE	★		★	★			
ILAM	★	★	★				
GRINDON				★			
BUTTERTON	★			★		★	
UPPER ELKSTONE				★			
UPPER HULME			★	★			
GRADBACH		★					
A537				★			
TAXAL				★			
BUXWORTH				★		★	
HAYFIELD	★		★				
LADYBOWER				★			
LONGSHAW				★			
BIRCHENS			★	★			
NORTHWOOD					★	★	
DARLEY BRG.	★		★	★		★	★

BED & BREAKFAST GUIDE

On or close to the route

MATLOCK	Crown Hotel, Crown Square. Tel: Matlock 2349
	Cavendish House, 26 Bank Road Tel: Matlock (0629) 2443
BONSALL	Sycamore Guest House, 76 High Street Tel: Wirksworth 3903
TISSINGTON	Bent Farm. Tel: Parwich 214
THORPE	The Old Orchard, Stoney Lane Tel: Thorpe Cloud 410
	Hillcrest House, Thorpe Tel: Thorpe Cloud (033529) 436
ILAM	Mrs E.M. Tuff, Town End Cottage, Ilam Tel: Thorpe Cloud (033529) 429
UPPER ELKSTONE	Mount Pleasant Farm. Tel: Blackshaw 380
UPPER HULME	Keekorak Lodge Farm. Tel: Blackshaw 218
KETTLESHULME	The Reed Farm. Tel: Whaley Bridge 2777
HAYFIELD	Tunstead Guest House, Kinder Tel: New Mills 42138
BAMFORD	Meadows Reach, 12 Main Street. Tel: Hope Valley 51216
BASLOW	Wheatsheaf Hotel. Tel: Baslow 2240
DARLEY BRIDGE	Square & Compass Inn Tel: Darley Dale 0629 733 255

YOUTH HOSTELS

MATLOCK
Bank Road, Matlock, Derbyshire, DE4 3NF.
Tel: Matlock (0629) 2983.

ILAM HALL
Ilam Hall, Ashbourne, Derbyshire, DE6 2AZ.
Tel: Thorpe Cloud (033529) 212.

GRADBACH MILL
Gradbach Mill, Gradbach, Quarnford, Buxton, Derbyshire, SK17 0SU.
Tel: Wincle (02607) 625

BUXTON
(5 miles from route)
Sherbrook Lodge, Harpur Hill Road,
Buxton, Derbyshire. SK17 9NB
Tel: Buxton (0298) 2287

EDALE
(1½ miles from route)
Rowland Cote, Nether Booth, Edale,
Sheffield, S30 2ZH.
Tel: Hope Valley (0433) 70302

HAGG FARM
Hagg Farm Hostel, Snake Road, Bamford,
Sheffield, S30 2BJ.
Tel: Hope Valley (0433) 51594
(Not a YHA hostel but run by the Peak Park Joint
Planning Board).

HATHERSAGE
(one mile off route)
Youth Hostel, Castleton Road, Hathersage,
Sheffield, S30 1AH.
Tel: Hope Valley (0433) 50493

THE MERMAID INN

CAMPING SITES
On or close to the route

MATLOCK	Packhorse Farm, Matlock Moor. Tel: Matlock 2781 G.R. SK322617
	Sycamore Farm. Tel: Matlock 55760 G.R. SK327616
THORPE	Highfield Farm Caravan Site. Tel: Thorpe Cloud 228 G.R. SK170510
ILAM	Garden Farm, Ilam Moor Lane. Tel: Thorpe Cloud 473 G.R. SK132513
UPPER HULME	Blackshaw Moor Caravan Club Site. Tel: Blackshaw 202/203 G.R. SK012603
HAYFIELD	Hayfield Campsite, Kinder Road. Tel: New Mills 45394 G.R. SK052875
HAGG FARM	Tel: Hope Valley 51594 G.R. SK161889 (Open June 1st - Sept. 30th. Closed Monday and Tuesday rest of year).
BASLOW	Eric Byne Memorial Campsite, Birchen Edge. Tel: Baslow 2277 G.R. SK278723
DARLEY BRIDGE	Square & Compass Inn Tel: 0629 733 255

LIST OF INNS
Actually passed on the route

MATLOCK	CROWN HOTEL
BONSALL	KING'S HEAD
BRASSINGTON	MINER'S ARMS. YE OLD GATE INN
THORPE	PEVERIL OF THE PEAK
ILAM	IZAAK WALTON HOTEL
GRINDON	CAVALIER INN
BUTTERTON	BLACK LION INN
NR. WARSLOW	MERMAID INN
UPPER HULME	ROCK INN
NR. BUXTON	CAT AND FIDDLE INN
TAXAL	CHIMES OF TAXAL
HORWICH END	JOLLY RODGER INN
BUXWORTH	NAVIGATION INN
ASHOPTON	LADYBOWER INN
LONGSHAW	FOX HOUSE INN. GROUSE INN
NR. BASLOW	ROBIN HOOD INN
DARLEY BRIDGE	SQUARE & COMPASS INN

LOG

Date Started ....

Date Completed ....

Route Point	Mile No.	Time		Comments/Weather
		Arr.	Dep.	
CROWN SQUARE	0			
MASSON LEES FARM	1			
BONSALL	2			
BONSALL MINES	3			
IBLE	4			
HARBORO ROCKS	5½			
BRASSINGTON	7			
BRADBOURNE	9			
BENT DUMBLE	10			
TISSINGTON	11			
HOLLINGTON END	12			
LIN DALE	13			
IZAAK WALTON	14			
ILAM Y.H.A.	15			
MUSDEN WOOD	16½			
CALTON	17½			
RIVER HAMPS	18½			
GRINDON	20½			
BUTTERTON	22½			
THE HILL	23			
RYECROFT	24			
NEW YORK	25			

LOG—continued

Route Point	Mile No.	Arr.	Dep.	Comments/Weather
MERMAID INN	26			
UPPER HULME	27½			
THE ROACHES	29			
GRADBACH Y.H.A.	31½			
3 SHIRES HEAD	34			
DANEBOWER	35			
CAT & FIDDLE INN	36½			
SHINING TOR	37½			
CATS TOR	39			
WINDGATHER	40½			
TAXAL	42			
HORWICH END	43			
BUXWORTH	44			
CHINLEY MOOR	46			
PHOSIDE FARM	47			
HAYFIELD CAMP	48			
EDALE CROSS	50			
PYM CHAIR	51			
UPPER TOR	53			
NETHER TOR	54			
MADWOMANSSTONES	55			
RIVER ASHOP	57			
HAGG FARM	57½			
CROOK HILL	59			
LADYBOWER INN	61			
MOSCAR	62			
STANAGE END	64			
TRIG 457	67			

LOG—continued

Route Point	Mile No.	Time Arr.	Dep.	Comments/Weather
HIGGER TOR	68			
SURPRISE VIEW	69			
LONGSHAW	70			
FROGGATT EDGE	72			
CURBAR EDGE	73			
EAGLE STONE	74			
A621	75			
BIRCHEN EDGE	76			
DOBB EDGE	78			
SWISS LAKE	79			
BEELEY HILL TOP	80½			
FALLANGE	83			
NORTHWOOD	84½			
CHURCHTOWN	86			
DARLEY BRIDGE	87			
MATLOCK	90			

NOTES:

TRAIL PROFILE
— Approx 10,500 feet of ascent.

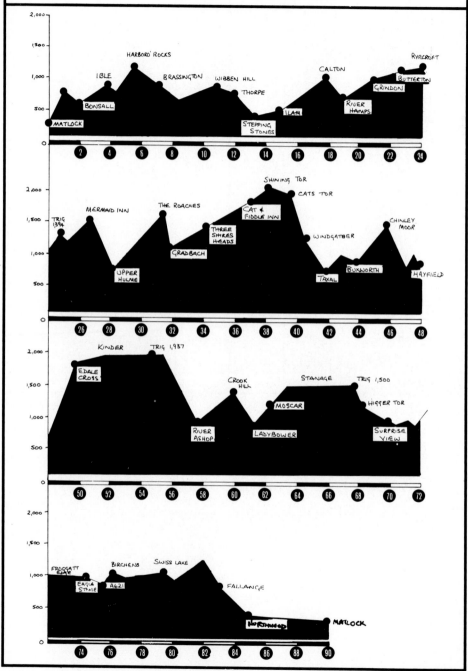

MAP SYMBOLS

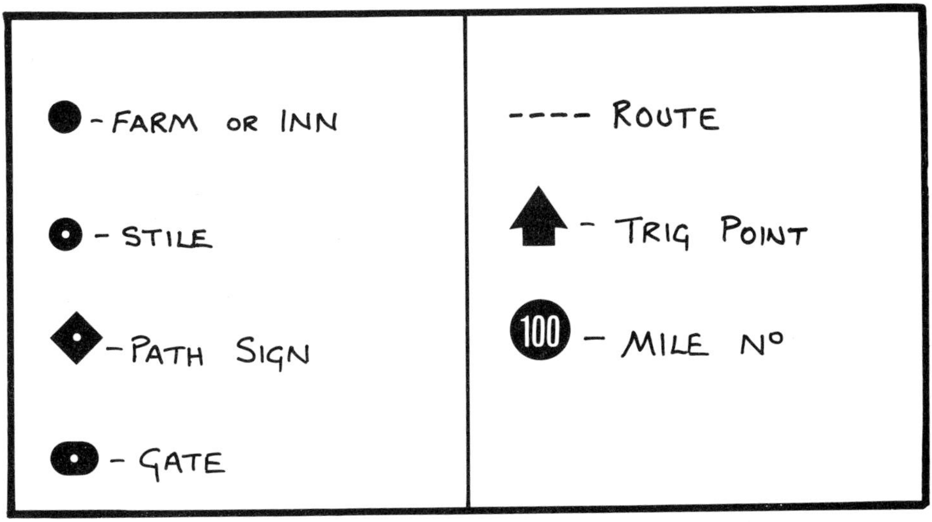

● – FARM OR INN

◉ – STILE

◆ – PATH SIGN

⬤ – GATE

---- ROUTE

▲ – TRIG POINT

⬤100 – MILE Nº

REMEMBER AND OBSERVE
THE COUNTRY CODE

ENJOY THE COUNTRYSIDE AND RESPECT ITS LIFE AND WORK.

GUARD AGAINST ALL RISK OF FIRE.

FASTEN ALL GATES.

KEEP YOUR DOGS UNDER CLOSE CONTROL.

KEEP TO PUBLIC PATHS ACROSS FARMLAND.

USE GATES AND STILES TO CROSS FENCES, HEDGES AND WALLS.

LEAVE LIVESTOCK, CROPS AND MACHINERY ALONE.

TAKE YOUR LITTER HOME—PACK IT IN, PACK IT OUT.

HELP TO KEEP ALL WATER CLEAN.

PROTECT WILDLIFE, PLANTS AND TREES.

TAKE SPECIAL CARE ON COUNTRY ROADS.

MAKE NO UNNECESSARY NOISE.

EQUIPMENT NOTES—some personal thoughts

BOOTS—preferably with a leather upper, of medium weight, with a vibram sole. I always add a foam cushioned insole to help cushion the base of my feet.

SOCKS—I generally wear two thick pairs as this helps to minimise blisters. The inner pair of loop stitch variety and approximately 80% wool. The outer a thick rib pair of approximately 80% wool.

WATERPROOFS—for general walking I wear a T shirt or shirt with a cotton wind jacket on top. You generate heat as you walk and I prefer to layer my clothes to avoid getting too hot. Depending on the season will dictate how many layers you wear. In soft rain I just use my wind jacket for I know it quickly dries out. In heavy downpours I slip on a neoprene lined cagoule, and although hot and clammy it does keep me reasonably dry. Only in extreme conditions will I don overtrousers, much preferring to get wet and feel comfortable.

FOOD—as I walk I carry bars of chocolate, for they provide instant energy and are light to carry. In winter a flask of hot coffee is welcome. I never carry water and find no hardship from doing so, but this is a personal matter. From experience I find the more I drink the more I want. You should always carry some extra food such as Kendal Mint Cake for emergencies.

RUCKSACK—for day walking I use a climbing rucksac of about 40 litre capacity and although excess space it does mean that the sac is well padded and with a shoulder strap. Inside apart from the basics for the day I carry gloves, balaclava, spare pullover and a pair of socks.

MAP & COMPASS—when I am walking I always have the relevant map—usually 1:25,000 scale—open in my hand. This enables me to constantly check that I am walking the right way. In case of bad weather I carry a Silva type compass, which once mastered gives you complete confidence in thick cloud or mist.

HIGH LEVEL

ROUTE

BADGE ORDER FORM

Date Completed ....

Time ....

Name ....

Address ....

Four colour embroided badge Price: £1.75 each, including signed certificate, postage and VAT.

From: J.N.M PUBLICATIONS, WINSTER, MATLOCK, DERBYSHIRE, DE4 2DQ.

OTHER BOOKS BY JOHN N. MERRILL PUBLISHED BY JNM PUBLICATIONS

DAY WALK GUIDES -

SHORT CIRCULAR WALKS IN THE PEAK DISTRICT
LONG CIRCULAR WALKS IN THE PEAK DISTRICT
CIRCULAR WALKS IN WESTERN PEAKLAND
SHORT CIRCULAR WALKS IN THE STAFFORDSHIRE MOORLANDS
PEAK DISTRICT TOWN WALKS
SHORT CIRCULAR WALKS AROUND MATLOCK
SHORT CIRCULAR WALKS IN THE DUKERIES
SHORT CIRCULAR WALKS IN SOUTH YORKSHIRE
CIRCULAR WALKS AROUND DERBY
HIKE TO BE FIT....STROLLING WITH JOHN
THE JOHN MERRILL WALK RECORD BOOK

CANAL WALK GUIDES -

VOL ONE—DERBYSHIRE AND NOTTINGHAMSHIRE
VOL TWO—CHESHIRE AND STAFFORDSHIRE

DAY CHALLENGE WALKS—

JOHN MERRILL'S PEAK DISTRICT CHALLENGE WALK
JOHN MERRILL'S YORKSHIRE DALES CHALLENGE WALK
JOHN MERRILL'S NORTH YORKSHIRE MOORS CHALLENGE WALK
PEAK DISTRICT END TO END WALKS
THE LITTLE JOHN CHALLENGE WALK
JOHN MERRILL'S LAKELAND CHALLENGE WALK

MULTIPLE DAY WALKS—

THE RIVERS' WAY
PEAK DISTRICT HIGH LEVEL ROUTE
PEAK DISTRICT MARATHONS
THE LIMEY WAY
THE PEAKLAND WAY

HISTORICAL GUIDES—

DERBYSHIRE INNS
100 HALLS AND CASTLES OF THE PEAK DISTRICT & DERBYSHIRE
TOURING THE PEAK DISTRICT AND DERBYSHIRE BY CAR
DERBYSHIRE FOLKLORE
LOST INDUSTRIES OF DERBYSHIRE
PUNISHMENT IN DERBYSHIRE
CUSTOMS OF THE PEAK DISTRICT AND DERBYSHIRE
WINSTER—A VISITOR'S GUIDE
ARKWRIGHT OF CROMFORD
TALES FROM THE MINES by GEOFFREY CARR

JOHN'S MARATHON WALKS—

TURN RIGHT AT LAND'S END
WITH MUSTARD ON MY BACK
TURN RIGHT AT DEATH VALLEY
EMERALD COAST WALK